Lessons from Aesop ~~~~~

Thank you for choosing to use these copywork pages with your child. The following pages are from Aesop for Children. Each fable has a corresponding lesson, and these pages are those lessons. There are 147 pages of copywork.

This copywork (labeled E for Elementary) is ideal for a young writer who has the basics down and is ready for lots of practice! The lines are 3/8 in tall with a dashed midline for extra guidance.

These pages are a perfect complement to your Ancient Greece studies, but are also great copywork pages for any child as they provide thought provoking lessons for your child to ponder as they write.

I would like to note that you may, personally, not agree with each of these lessons. Please use your discretion before assigning your child a copywork page. With almost 150 pages to choose from, I am sure you will find the vast majority of them to be agreeable. (I included all of them because I know each family is unique.)

Copywork is a fantastic way to help your child master reading, penmanship, grammar, and spelling all at the same time, simply and subtly. I hope you and your child enjoy using this copywork pack together!

Amy @ www.classicalcopywork.com

from – The Wolf and the Kid

Do not let anything turn

you from your purpose.

Foolish curiosity and

vanity often lead to

misfortune.

from – The Young Crab and His Mother

Do not tell others how

to act unless you can

set a good example.

Do not attempt the

impossible.

from – The Dog, the Rooster, and the Fox

Those who try to

deceive may expect to

be paid in their own

coin.

It is one thing to say

that something should

be done, but quite a

different matter to do it.

8   www.classicalcopywork.com

from – The Eagle and the Jackdaw

Do not let your vanity

make you overestimate

your powers.

Do not attempt too

much at once.

Can you draw a picture to go with this fable?

10   www.classicalcopywork.com

from – Hercules and the Wagoner

lesson 1

Self help is the best

help.

lesson 2

Heaven helps those who

help themselves.

Do not say anything at

any time that you would

not say at all times.

from – The Town Mouse and the Country Mouse

Poverty with security is

better than plenty in

the midst of fear and

uncertainty.

There are many who

pretend to despise and

belittle that which is

beyond their reach.

from – The Bundle of Sticks

In unity is strength.

Can you draw a picture to go with this fable?

Expect no reward for

serving the wicked.

from – The Donkey and His Driver

They who will not listen

to reason but stubbornly

go their own way

against the friendly

advice of those who are

wiser than they, are on

the road to misfortune.

They complain most who

suffer least.

Can you draw a picture to go with this fable?

from – The Lion and the Mouse

A kindness is never

wasted.

Liars are not believed

even when they speak

the truth.

from – The Gnat and the Bull

lesson 1

We are often of greater

importance in our own

eyes than in the eyes

of our neighbor.

lesson 2

The smaller the mind

the greater the conceit.

Our best blessings are

often the least

appreciated.

from – The Farmer and the Stork

You are judged by the

company you keep.

It is easy to be brave

when there is no

danger.

from – The Travelers and the Purse

We cannot expect

anyone to share our

misfortunes unless we

are willing to share our

good fortune also.

Do not resent the

remarks of a fool.

Ignore them.

Can you draw a picture to go with this fable?

from – The Frogs who Wished for a King

Be sure you can better

your condition before

you seek to change.

lesson 1

Flattery is not a proof

of true admiration.

lesson 2

Do not let flattery throw

you off your guard

against an enemy.

from – The Wolf and his Shadow

Do not let your fancy

make you forget

realities.

Better to yield when it

is folly to resist, than to

resist stubbornly and be

destroyed.

from – The Rat and the Elephant

A resemblance to the

great in some things

does not make us great.

Can you draw a picture to go with this fable?

Always stop to think

whether your fun may

not be the cause of

another's unhappiness.

from – The Crow and the Pitcher

In a pinch a good use

of our wits may help us

out.

from – The Ants and the Grasshopper

There's a time for work

and a time for play.

www.classicalcopywork.com

from – The Donkey Carrying the Image

Do not try to take the

credit to yourself that

is due to others.

Can you draw a picture to go with this fable?

A change of habits will

not alter nature.

from – The Two Goats

It is better to yield than

to come to misfortune

through stubbornness.

The same measures will

not suit all

circumstances.

from – The Lion and the Gnat

lesson 1

The least of our enemies

is often the most to be

feared.

lesson 2

Pride over a success

should not throw us off

our guard.

Deeds count, not

boasting words.

Can you draw a picture to go with this fable?

from – The Rooster and the Jewel

Precious things are

without value to those

who cannot prize them.

Can you draw a picture to go with this fable?

Do not try to ape your

betters.

from – The Wild Boar and the Fox

Preparedness for war is

the best guarantee of

peace.

from – The Donkey, the Fox, and the Lion

Traitors may expect

treachery.

Can you draw a picture to go with this fable?

from – The Birds, the Beasts, and the Bat

The deceitful have no

friends.

Can you draw a picture to go with this fable?

from – The Lion, the Bear, and the Fox

Those who have all the

toil do not always get

the profit.

from – The Wolf and the Lamb

lesson 1

The tyrant can always

find an excuse for his

tyranny.

lesson 2

The unjust will not listen

to the reasoning of the

innocent.

A knave's hypocrisy is

easily seen through.

Can you draw a picture to go with this fable?

from – The Hares and the Frogs

However unfortunate we

may think we are there

is always someone worse

off than ourselves.

Do not play tricks on

your neighbors unless

you can stand the same

treatment yourself.

from – The Travelers and the Sea

Do not let your hopes

carry you away from

reality.

Can you draw a picture to go with this fable?

What is evil won is evil

lost.

from – The Stag and His Reflection

We often make much of

the ornamental and

despise the useful.

Do not sacrifice your

freedom for the sake of

pomp and show.

from – The Mice and the Weasels

Greatness has its

penalities.

lesson 1

Do not depend on the

promises of those whose

interest it is to deceive

you.

lesson 2

Take what you can get

when you can get it.

from – The Fox and the Lion

lesson 1

Familiarity breeds

contempt.

lesson 2

Acquaintance with evil

blinds us to its dangers.

The loud-mouthed

boaster does not impress

nor frighten those who

know him.

from – The Dog and his Master's Dinner

Do not stop to argue

with temptation.

Can you draw a picture to go with this fable?

Borrowed feathers do

not make fine birds.

from – The Monkey and the Dolphin

One falsehood leads to

another.

Stick to your trade.

from – The Monkey and the Cat

The flatterer seeks some

benefit at your expense.

It is easy and also

contemptible to kick a

man that is down.

Can you draw a picture to go with this fable?

from – The Dogs and the Hides

Do not try to do

impossible things.

The strong are apt to

settle questions to their

own advantage.

Can you draw a picture to go with this fable?

from – The Bear and the Bees

It is wiser to bear a

single injury in silence

than to provoke a

thousand by flying into

a rage.

A fine coat is not

always an indication of

an attractive mind.

from – The Heron

Do not be too hard to

suit or you may have to

be content with the

worst or with nothing

at all.

The trickster is easily

tricked.

Can you draw a picture to go with this fable?

www.classicalcopywork.com

from – The Dog in the Manger

Do not grudge others

what you cannot enjoy

yourself.

An invitation prompted

by selfishness is not to

be accepted.

from – The Donkey and the Grasshoppers

The laws of nature are

unchangeable.

Can you draw a picture to go with this fable?

Be sure of your

pedigree before you

boast of it.

Can you draw a picture to go with this fable?

from – The Fox and the Goat

Look before you leap.

from – The Cat, the Rooster, and the Young Mouse

Do not trust alone in

outward appearances.

from – The Wolf and the Shepherd

Once a wolf, always a

wolf.

The useful is of much

more importance and

value, than the

ornamental.

from – The Farmer and the Cranes

lesson 1

Bluff and threatening

words are of little value

with rascals.

lesson 2

Bluff is no proof that

hard fists are lacking.

Industry is itself a

treasure.

from – The Two Pots

Equals make the best

friends.

Those who have plenty

want more and so lose

all they have.

from – The Fighting Bulls and the Frog

When the great fall out,

the weak must suffer

for it.

Greediness leads to

misfortune.

Can you draw a picture to go with this fable?

from – The Farmer and the Snake

Learn from my fate not

to take pity on a

scoundrel.

Can you draw a picture to go with this fable?

Good will is worth

nothing unless it is

accompanied by good

acts.

from – The Goatheard and the Wild Goats

It is unwise to treat old

friends badly for the

sake of new ones.

One swallow does not

make a summer.

from – The Cat and the Birds

Be wise and shun the

quack.

Can you draw a picture to go with this fable?

Act in haste and repent

at leisure – and often in

pain.

Can you draw a picture to go with this fable?

from – The Astrologer

Take care of the little

things and the big

things will take care of

themselves.

from – The Bullocks and a Lion

In unity is strength.

from –Mercury and the Woodman

Honesty is the best

policy.

Those who seek to harm

others often come to

harm themselves through

their own deceit.

from – The Fox and the Crab

Be content with your lot.

An act of kindness is

well repaid.

from – The Wolf in Sheep's Clothing

The evil doer often

comes to harm through

his own deceit.

It is wicked to take

advantage of another's

distress.

from – The Eagle and the Beetle

Even the weakest may

find means to avenge

a wrong.

Take warning from the

misfortunes of others.

from – The Man and the Lion

It all depends on the

point of view, and who

tells the story.

lesson 1

Behavior that is

regarded as agreeable

in one is very rude and

impertinent in another.

from – The Donkey and the Lap Dog

lesson 2

Do not try to gain favor

by acting in a way that

is contrary to your own

nature and character.

Do not count your

chickens before they

are hatched.

from – The Wolf and the Shepherd

Men often condem

others for what they see

no wrong in doing

themselves.

Wicked deeds will not

stay hid.

from – The Miser

A possession is worth no

more than the use we

make of it.

There is nothing worth

so much as liberty.

from – The Fox and the Hedgehog

Better to bear a lesser

evil than to risk a

greater in removing it.

Set your sails with the

wind.

from – The Quack Toad

Those who would mend

others, should first mend

themselves.

Do not listen to the

advice of him who

seeks to lower you to

his own level.

from – The Mischievous Dog

Notoriety is not fame.

Do not expect

consistancy in others if

you have none yourself.

from – The Cat and the Fox

Common sense is always

worth more than

cunning.

Whatever you do, do

with all your might.

from – The Old Lion

It is cowardly to attack

the defenseless, though

he be an enemy.

Too much attention to

danger may cause us to

fall victims to it.

from – Two Travelers and a Bear

Misfortune is the test of

true friendship.

Give a finger and lose

a hand.

from – The Fox and the Monkey

The true leader proves

himself by his qualities.

Do not believe

everything you hear.

from – The Flies and the Honey

Be not greedy for a

little passing pleasure.

It may destroy you.

from – The Eagle and the Kite

Everything is fair in love.

from – The Stag, the Sheep, and the Wolf

Two blacks do not make

a white.

The weak are made to

suffer for the misdeeds

of the powerful.

from – The Shepherd and the Lion

lesson 1

We are often not so

eager for what we seek,

after we have found it.

lesson 2

Do not foolishly ask for

things that would bring

ruin if they were granted.

It is very foolish to be

greedy.

from – The Hare and the Tortoise

The race is not always

to the swift.

Ability proves itself by

deeds.

from – The Lark and her Young Ones

Self-help is the best

help.

The wise do not let

themselves be tricked a

second time.

from – The Fox and the Crow

The flatterer lives at the

expense of those who

will listen to him.

In quarreling about the

shadow we often lose

the substance.

Lessons from Aesop ~~~~~

from – The Miller, his Son, and the Donkey

If you try to please all,

you please none.

A kindness is never

wasted.

from – The Man and the Satyr

The man who talks for

both sides is not to be

trusted by either.

from – The Wolf, the Kid, and the Goat

Two sureties are better

than one.

www.classicalcopywork.com

from – The Swallow and the Crow

Friends in fine weather

only, are not worth

much.

from – Jupiter and the Plague

Mother love is blind.

www.classicalcopywork.com

from – The Lion, the Donkey, and the Fox

Learn from the

misfortunes of others.

Might makes right.

from – The Mole and his Mother

Boast of one thing and

you will be found

lacking in that and a

few other things as well.

Gentleness and kind

persuasion win where

force and bluster fail.

from – The Hare and his Ears

Your enemies will seize

any excuse to attack

you.

Do not give up friends

for foes.

from – The Rooster and the Fox

The wicked deserve no

aid.

A fool may deceive by

his dress and

appearance, but his

words will soon show

what he really is.

from – The Fisherman and the Little Sun

A small gain is worth

more than a large

promise.

from – The Fighting Roosters and the Eagle

Pride goes before a fall.

www.classicalcopywork.com

Lessons from Aesop ~~~~~

This copywork pack has been created by Amy Maze.

Hi, I'm Amy! I am a homemaker, mother, child of God, blogger, and owner of Classical Copywork. I love to learn, plan, and create. When I am not teaching my children or spending time with my husband, you will find me blogging at Living and Learning at Home and creating new copywork packs like this one!

www.classicalcopywork.com

Would you like a free page of copywork sent to your email every week?

Would you like discount codes for copywork packs?

Visit www.classicalcopywork.com to sign up to receive one free copywork page and one discount code each week.

As a bonus for subscribing, you will receive the Classical Copywork Sampler!

"Sample pages from each copywork pack at Classical Copywork, packaged together in one convenient download!"

Did you enjoy this copywork pack?

Then you might enjoy...

Is your child ready for the next level of copywork? Check out these...

Made in the USA
Coppell, TX
19 March 2021